The Rehearsal

OR

Living Life Live

By Randy Walter

The Rehearsal

Copyright © 2015 by Shiloh Ministries, Inc.

ISBN 978-0-9890789-1-7

Published by Shiloh Ministries, Inc., in January, 2015

> Scripture quotations marked "ASV" are from the *American Standard Version Bible*, public domain.
>
> Scripture quotations marked "CEB" are from the *Common English Bible®*, copyright 2011. Used by permission. All rights reserved.
>
> Scripture quotations marked "CEV" are from the *Contemporary English Version* © 1991, 1992, 1995 by American Bible Society. Used by Permission.
>
> Scripture quotations marked "KJV" are taken from *The King James Version of the Holy Bible*, public domain.
>
> Scripture quotations marked "NASB" are taken from *The New American Standard Bible®*, Copyright © 1960, 1962, 1963, 1968, 1971, 1972, 1973, 1975, 1977, 1995 by The Lockman Foundation. Used by permission.
>
> Scripture quotations marked "NIV" are taken from the *Holy Bible, New International Version®*. Copyright © 1973, 1978, 1984 by International Bible Society. Used by permission of Zondervan. All rights reserved.
>
> Scripture quotations marked "NKJV" are taken from the *New King James Version*. Copyright © 1982 by Thomas Nelson, Inc. Used by permission. All rights reserved.
>
> Scripture quotations marked "NLT" are taken from the *Holy Bible, New Living Translation*, copyright © 1996. Used by permission of Tyndale House Publishers, Inc., Wheaton, IL 60189 USA. All rights reserved.
>
> Scripture quotations marked "RSV" are taken from *The Revised Standard Version of the Bible*, copyright 1989 by the Division of Christian Education of the National Council of the Churches of Christ in the USA. Used by permission. All rights reserved.
>
> Scripture quotations marked "TLB" are taken from *The Living Bible*, copyright © 1971. Used by permission of Tyndale House Publishers, Inc., Carol Stream, Illinois 60188. All rights reserved.

All rights reserved. This book is protected by the copyright laws of the United States of America, and may not be copied or reprinted for commercial use or profit. No part of this book may be reproduced or transmitted in any form or by any means – electronic, mechanical or photographic – including photocopying, recording or by any information storage and retrieval system, without prior written permission of the publisher. No patent liability is assumed with respect to the use of the information contained herein. The publisher and authors assume no responsibility for errors or omissions; neither is any liability assumed for damages resulting from use of the information contained herein.

Printed in the United States of America.

The Rehearsal

This Book Belongs to

_____

Presented by

_____

BOOK ORDERS

***The Rehearsal* or Living Life Live** – Additional copies of this 48-page booklet are available for **$10 each** *(includes shipping)*.

Things Hoped For – 25 years of prophetic wisdom and encounters with God – two books in one – 304 pages. Readers are saying—

"It is the most profoundly faith-building book I have ever read."

"It was delightfully refreshing, enlightening, and very sobering."

"…a good book to purchase for people who are struggling with their Christian walk."

"…an honest portrayal of the walk of faith."

"Excellent resource for intercessory prayer..."

Special price $10 each *(includes shipping)*.

Timeless Wisdom series of messages recorded as they were received them from the Lord – 48 pages each on three different themes. **Three-booklet set is $10** *(includes shipping)*.

| Kingdom Living | Prosperous Living | Revival Living |

Send checks to:
Shiloh Ministries, 209 West St., Berlin, MD 21811
ThingsHopedFor@comcast.net

The Rehearsal

Contents

Chapter 1	Life is a Rehearsal	1
Chapter 2	A Man-pleasing Spirit	6
Chapter 3	Childlike Faith	9
Chapter 4	The Shroud of Shame	13
Chapter 5	Rehearsing vs. Planning	17
Chapter 6	Living Life Live	22
Chapter 7	Courage for the Kingdom	25
Chapter 8	Doorway to Your First Love	28
Chapter 9	Worrying is Rehearsing	31
Chapter 10	A Personal Note	37

Chapter 1

Life is a Rehearsal

When you think of rehearsing, what comes to mind? An orchestra practicing for a concert? Actors rehearsing a play?

What about rehearsing life itself – living it in our minds before it unfolds in our days? Isn't all of life a rehearsal for the life to come?

I considered rehearsing a sophisticated form of preparation until the Lord told me to **"stop rehearsing the future."** He wasn't forbidding me to make plans or have vision. He gave me this instruction because insecurity prompted me to rehearse life's events ahead of time in an attempt to control them. I was robbing myself of the peace and stability which come from trusting Him.

This instruction prompted me to search my soul and recognize how pervasive rehearsing was in my approach to living. I perceived the many different ways in which I rehearsed, discovering more of them nearly every day.

The Rehearsal or **Living Life Live**

I understood how rehearsing stunted the growth of my faith. I became aware of areas where I was not open to God while rehearsing. Rather than squander my spiritual strength on fear and control, I am learning how to surrender and seek His peace.

Proverbs 3:5-6 (NKJV) took on greater meaning for me—

"Trust in the Lord with all your heart, and lean not on your own understanding; in all your ways acknowledge Him, and He shall direct your paths."

Writing this booklet has been an exercise in not rehearsing. The Lord said He would download it, and all I had to do was be a reporter. He didn't dictate it word for word, as I thought at first. Rather, He directed my thinking to write what He wanted said.

After a lifetime of rehearsing the future, I am now experiencing the spontaneity of the Holy Spirit. It is a joyful relief. The Lord asked me to publish *The Rehearsal* so you can experience it too.

WHAT WE REHEARSE

Think of all the ways we rehearse.

We rehearse by imagining ourselves doing the things we want to accomplish before we do them.

If we want to learn something, we repeat it to ourselves, rehearsing the knowledge we wish to acquire until it is committed to memory.

As a new Christian, I heard a teaching so powerful that I have attempted to rehearse it to this day: When we account

Chapter 1 – Life is a Rehearsal

for our lives before God, what will He look for in us? He will search to see if we resemble His Son. Knowing I have no righteousness of my own, I want God to see the imputed righteousness of Christ because I look like Him.

So, like many Christians, I rehearse being like Jesus by reading the Scriptures and memorizing His words, looking ahead to the day when we will be transformed into His image.

"For whom He foreknew, He also predestined to be conformed to the image of His Son…" (Romans 8:29 NKJV).

We alter our daily behavior to comply with His nature, hoping God sees the likeness of Jesus when we appear before Him.

"…It has not yet been revealed what we shall be, but we know that when He is revealed, we shall be like Him…" (I John 3:2 NKJV).

REHEARSING FAITH

John Wesley, with his brother Charles and evangelist George Whitefield, started the Methodist movement, which was instrumental in The First Great Awakening in the American colonies. Yet early in his life, a disillusioned John Wesley returned to England from Savannah, Georgia, doubting his very faith and salvation. He wrote in his journal, "I who went to America to convert others was never myself converted to God."

In London, Wesley met Peter Böhler, a Moravian missionary to the Americas. He asked Böhler if he should leave

The Rehearsal or **Living Life Live**

the pulpit, and Böhler answered, "By no means."

Wesley retorted, "But what can I preach?" Then Böhler gave the momentous reply, "Preach faith till you have it; and then, because you have it, you will preach faith."

In essence, Böhler told Wesley to rehearse faith until it became so ingrained that he would naturally spread it to others. Böhler's words have resounded for centuries.

Where faith is concerned, rehearsing is a good thing. That is why it was such a surprise when the Lord told me to *"stop rehearsing the future."* The understanding which followed opened my mind to a downside of rehearsing life.

REHEARSING POVERTY

As I became increasingly aware of the ways in which I rehearse, the Lord told me I was **"rehearsing poverty."** It was true. The extent of my vision for living was reduced to "getting by." I saw Him as "the God of barely enough" rather than "the Lord of abundance and extravagant generosity."

For decades I had prayed from III John that I will prosper and be in health as my soul prospers. I always took that to mean, as my soulish nature obeys God and He approves of me, prosperity and good health will follow. He showed me that for my soul to prosper means more than obedience. My soul needs to rehearse prosperity as an expression of trust in Him, then other things will follow in season.

The Lord told my wife, Barbara, and me that as we hope all things (per I Corinthians 13:7), we rehearse success. He instructed us to keep reminding ourselves of all we have to be

Chapter 1 – Life is a Rehearsal

thankful for by stating, *"Gratitude creates an atmosphere for increase."*

It was a huge shift in my thinking, away from the false meekness of believing God will toss me a few crumbs to keep me alive, and to the assurance that He is able to do exceedingly abundantly above all I can ask or think (Ephesians 3:20 NKJV). The end of that scripture says, **"according to the power that works in us,"** which is the faith that He loves us and has our best interest at heart.

"GOD IS LOVE"

The root of all fear is, "God does not love me."

Tension between fear and faith is the fulcrum of our existence. When the Bible talks about overcoming, it refers to victory in this conflict.

In his first epistle, John wrote, **"God is love"** (4:8 NKJV). No other passage in Scripture captures God's nature so exactly and succinctly.

Chapter 2

A Man-pleasing Spirit

I like being prepared. Whether it's a speaking engagement or a telephone conversation, I would rehearse my words ahead of time to achieve the maximum effect.

When I started a journalism career at age 18, one of the most intimidating things I encountered was speaking over the phone. I feared I was too young to be taken seriously, that I had no influence, that I couldn't get the job done. But I discovered my voice had favor, and good phone presence was a helpful tool. Sometimes I could persuade people by phone more than in person.

Coming to the point quickly was most effective. I carefully scripted myself, planning each word I would say. It seemed the more I rehearsed, the less opportunity others had to object or refuse. This was intended not as overt manipulation but to win people to whatever cause I was calling about. It was a snapshot of my outlook on life. I thought that the

Chapter 2 – A Man-pleasing Spirit

better my anticipation of things to come, the better I could achieve the desired result.

PRESUMPTION

In high school I joined the Demosthenes Debating Society. Debaters across the country were given a single topic and assigned to teams of two, which would argue for or against it in weekly matches with other schools. It was a great exercise in research and presentation. In two years, my team only lost once.

To overcome what I assumed were the predictable positions of our opponents, I created a punch list of their anticipated points and my responses, so I could refute their arguments. It was a rehearsal for the purpose of control.

I didn't realize how lazy and presumptuous my rehearsing was until we met the team which beat us. They were better prepared and more confident because they studied the subject in depth, rather than merely developing a formula for arguing their case.

I was interested in appearances rather than mastering the topic. My confidence came from believing I was smarter than other people and could second-guess their thinking.

Presumption is part of rehearsing. It works sometimes, but not always. Presumption reinforces a sense of control, which always sets the stage for disappointment.

FEAR OF MAN

As I grew older, to be safe from criticism and surprises, I tried to figure out everything ahead of time. I rehearsed the

The Rehearsal or **Living Life Live**

future so I could control it and not feel bad about myself. This was rooted in the fear of man which produces a man-pleasing spirit.

Proverbs 29:25 (NLT) says, **"Fearing people is a dangerous trap, but trusting the Lord means safety."**

Rehearsing obstructed my faith. It even kept me from being creative. It replaced healthy excitement with routine.

Instead of anticipating things ahead of time, God wanted me to be confident in His direction for me. When He told me to *"stop rehearsing the future,"* it was a call to trust Him completely.

Childlike Faith

Trusting in the Lord requires faith. Paul wrote that every man is given **"the measure of faith"** (Romans 12:3 KJV), but we still have to activate it. "Childlike" faith is trusting God to the exclusion of our natural senses and human reasoning.

Jesus said only people who become like little children will enter the Kingdom of Heaven. What kind of faith does a small child possess? Little children are innocent. Their nature is trusting and believing, loving and forgiving, and not worried about what may happen later.

When introduced to a new environment with other children their own age, they automatically gravitate to one another. They interact without the apprehension adults frequently bring into social settings, like fear of inadequacy or rejection. Little children are naturally themselves. They have not yet learned to cater to the expectations of others.

Little children live in the moment. They often fail to think ahead or anticipate consequences. Their world is

The Rehearsal or **Living Life Live**

wrapped up in their present activity.

For adults, faith usually dwells in the shadow of things to come. The Bible's classic definition of faith puts it in a future context, calling it **"the substance of things hoped for, the evidence of things not seen"** (Hebrews 11:1 KJV).

By saying to be like a little child, Jesus taught us to live in the present moment and trust God without fear of the future. Rehearsing is a distraction from the present. Rehearsing keeps us from experiencing God's love and generosity as we envision self-reliant outcomes, even to everyday tasks. Rehearsing is being self-conscious. God wants us to be God-confident, not self-conscious.

GOD IS IN THE NOW

"Seek the Lord while He may be found. Call upon Him now while He is near," pleaded the prophet Isaiah (Isaiah 55:6 NKJV).

One of God's attributes is omnipresence – He is everywhere. King David wrote, **"If I ascend into heaven, You are there; if I make my bed in hell, behold, You are there"** (Psalm 139:8 NKJV).

Rather than ask *where* to seek Him, a better question might be *when* to seek Him – not what time of the day or the week, but in the past, present or future. God is eternal; He exists in every dimension of time. But we are only capable of encountering Him in the present.

For some people it is easier to dwell in the past, reliving old triumphs and pleasant memories to escape a reality that

Chapter 3 - Childlike Faith

is painful or empty. Others avoid the present by planning or predicting the future. An old adage says, "Sorrow looks back. Worry looks ahead. Faith looks up."

Faith brings closure to a man's corrupt nature by opening his senses to God's presence. The Bible says He reveals Himself through all Creation. A man can observe God's fingerprints in the world around him and on the lives of people He has touched. Faith is how a man recognizes God.

God wants us to know Him by coming into a relationship with Him, not by trying to imagine what He might be like. He wants us to live by faith – trusting Him even when we don't understand His methods or our circumstances.

WORRY ABOUT TOMORROW

In His Sermon on the Mount, Jesus said anxiety over the future is detrimental and unspiritual. **"Therefore do not worry about tomorrow…"** (Matthew 6:34 NKJV). Rather, He said to pursue the things of God's Kingdom and seek to be righteous; then God will meet all our needs. If we dwell in peace, trusting God instead of fretting over what may happen, He will take care of us. This is how little children instinctively live, unless they learn otherwise.

How practical is that for a grown-up? How can someone with adult responsibilities have the faith of a little child? Jesus was not saying to avoid thinking ahead or planning for the future; He warned against what He called **"the cares of this world"** (Matthew 13:22 NKJV). Cares often involve fear of the future, and can become so overwhelming that they draw men away from God. That is why Peter wrote, **"Cast all your**

The Rehearsal or Living Life Live

anxieties on Him, for He cares about you" (I Peter 5:7 RSV).

Doing this means exchanging sophistication, worry and control for the restoration of lost innocence. It is a high price for people whose worldly ambition defines them by position and influence; but a childlike nature can be reclaimed by anyone who learns to trust God instead of himself.

That was the case with Nicodemus, the Pharisee who visited Jesus secretly because he was afraid it would cost him his standing among the Jewish leaders. He came to express support, but was taken off guard when Jesus said, **"'I tell you the truth, unless you are born again, you cannot see the Kingdom of God.'**

"'What do you mean?' exclaimed Nicodemus. 'How can an old man go back into his mother's womb and be born again?'" (John 3:3-4 NLT).

Jesus was not talking about physical rebirth but spiritual regeneration – regaining the pure faith of a little child. Being born again is giving up our right to ourselves and surrendering to God so He can restore our innocence.

The Shroud of Shame

On the surface, "innocence" seems like a simple concept – until viewed through the lens of shame. The enemy of our souls keeps us from receiving God's love, acceptance and restoration by using shame, unworthiness and false guilt. Of these three weapons, shame is the most powerful.

For my entire lifetime, shame was a deep-rooted presence. When I became aware of it, I thought shame was the result of the shameful things I did. Regrets trapped me in the past, not due to missed opportunities or personal losses but because of terrible things I had done to other people. Whenever I remembered them, the shroud of shame covered me again.

Even after I became a Christian, shame tainted my self-image and distorted my outlook. Shame used the label "victim" to defend itself. Worst of all, shame declared, "This is the way it is. It can never change. Your whole life will be this way."

The Rehearsal or **Living Life Live**

Then a conference on deliverance helped me realize that my shame was not from things I did. Shame was there before I did those things. Because I was ashamed, I did shameful things.

I wondered how shame gained access to my life. Immediately I thought back to a one-time experience at the age of four, when my mother did something lewd and indecent with me. It didn't interfere with our relationship, but I never forgot it. That was where shame entered.

THE ORPHAN

Shame is the hallmark of the orphan spirit. A person with that spirit doesn't know how to receive love from other people or the Heavenly Father. He lives in fear – anticipating rejection, insecure about intimacy, expecting failure and abandonment, anxious about provision and protection. He is critical and condemning toward himself and others, feels out of place and alone, lacks vision for the future, and harbors anger.

Lucifer was the first orphan. Now he tries to deny the work of the cross and the blood of Jesus by persuading us, "Your fate is the same as mine." He uses fear to convince us.

All fear comes from the fear that God does not love us and is not faithful to us. In my case, agreeing out of ignorance produced fear of the future, which compelled me to rehearse it.

It insults God when we act like orphans, as though we were refusing His Gift of adoption.

Chapter 4 – The Shroud of Shame

"You didn't receive a spirit of slavery to lead you back again into fear, but you received a Spirit that shows you are adopted as His children. With this Spirit, we cry, 'Abba, Father'" (Romans 8:15 CEB).

HIDING

Years before that deliverance conference, while sitting dignified and smug in church one Sunday morning, I heard a quiet voice say in my spirit, *"You're hiding in here."* I knew exactly what the Lord meant. I was trying to look spiritual while ignoring important things He had given me to do.

Fear of man had prompted me to hide for my entire life. I hid from leadership and accomplishment, from honesty and accountability, from letting myself be known. It was the fruit of an orphan mind-set.

The shroud of shame made me passive to avoid disappointing others and feeling bad about myself. Subconsciously, I thought that if I didn't assert myself, I wouldn't be rejected. Shame fed a man-pleasing spirit.

God wanted me to be free from shame so I would walk in greater authority and complete the work He assigned to me.

SOUL TIE TO SHAME

I had a soul tie to shame – an unhealthy emotional dependence on it which undermined my relationships with other people and with God. Shame from that childhood episode caused me to resist authority and dishonor women – another lifelong pattern which needed to be broken.

The Rehearsal or **Living Life Live**

During the week after the conference, I realized that I needed to forgive my mother, even though she died 40 years earlier. And I needed to repent for my part in that incident. It did not matter whether it was something I did or something done to me. Barbara supported me as I prayed.

Although I held no unforgiveness, I forgave. I repented for participating and for being ashamed. Repentance is more than being sorry, apologizing and asking to be pardoned; it is changing one's way of thinking, which results in a change of behavior. I did not want to be ashamed any longer.

Barbara sensed an immediate difference in me as I adjusted to the absence shame which had affected me for as long as I could remember. It was as if I once again became a new creation in Christ (II Corinthians 5:17).

I was able to understand what God meant when He instructed Barbara and me to *"think big, look long."* Living without fear helped me embrace vision for my life and our ministry.

The Lord explained to us:

"Shame is part of the guilt over sin which is washed away by the blood of Jesus every time you ask to be forgiven.

"If you feel shame over areas you've already confessed to Me, that's not the conviction of My Spirit. It is an effective weapon in the hands of the enemy."

Chapter 5

Rehearsing vs. Planning

Did restoring my childlike innocence and living in the present mean I should no longer plan ahead? Not at all. Planning is part of vision, and without vision there is no life. Solomon wrote, **"Where there is no vision, the people perish..."** (Proverbs 29:18 KJV).

It is possible to make plans and still let God be in control. Solomon also wrote, **"The mind of man plans his way, but the Lord directs his steps"** (Proverbs 16:9 NASB). I had to learn to distinguish between planning to achieve and rehearsing to control.

Since elementary school, I have made plans by keeping lists. This helps me remember obligations, recognize priorities, work more efficiently, and enjoy a sense of accomplishment when I check things off. These are plans for success.

The Bible says we should plan ahead. **"For which of you, intending to build a tower, does not sit down first and count the cost, whether he has enough to finish it...?"** (Luke 14:28 NKJV).

The Rehearsal or Living Life Live

When we plan for success, sometimes we actually rehearse it in our minds. Take everyday physical activities which require judgment – throwing, stacking, steering, etc. Whether we know it or not, we first imagine these things happening the way we wish, then conform our efforts to the desired outcome. Sports and music are good examples of practice as a valid form of rehearsing success.

We can also unwittingly plan for failure by rehearsing problems. Whatever we rehearse, we enable; and whatever we fear, we invite. Job said, **"What I feared has come upon me…"** (Job 3:25 NIV). Rehearsing problems nurtures fear, resentment and a victim mentality.

While we need to remain aware of a problem, rehearsing the solution paves the way for faith, favor and advancement. In any situation, it is important to rehearse the solution, not the problem.

THE PROPHETIC

The prophetic is a form of rehearsing. Genuine prophecy, rooted in truth and wisdom, should help us plan for success. Whether it foretells the future or instructs in individual righteousness, it is personal encouragement that recognizes our circumstances and increases our faith in areas where we need to overcome.

Since the Fall of Man, we have wanted to know what lies ahead because it reveals our fate and provides a sense of power. God does not intend prophecy to feed an insecure need to know and manipulate the future. When we strive for foreknowledge, the enemy of our souls tempts us with pro-

Chapter 5 - Rehearsing Vs. Planning

fane methods of predicting the future as a way to skirt God's sovereignty.

From ancient soothsayers to modern psychics, people have devised carnal techniques to tell what lies ahead. God calls this "divination," which includes defiling ourselves with mediums and familiar spirits. He warns, **"I will set My face against that person and cut him off from his people"** (Leviticus 20:6 NKJV).

Prophecy, on the other hand, is when God Himself reveals the future. It might be the promise of a blessing. People can live for such promises. Take Simeon. God promised him that he would not die before seeing the Messiah, and he anticipated the fulfillment of this promise every day.

At the time of Jesus' dedication in the temple, Simeon held the infant in his arms and proclaimed, **"Sovereign Lord, as You have promised, You may now dismiss Your servant in peace. For my eyes have seen Your salvation, which You have prepared in the sight of all nations: a light for revelation to the Gentiles, and the glory of Your people Israel"** (Luke 2:29-32 NIV).

Sometimes prophecy is a merciful warning from God that people must change or suffer loss. In the account of Jonah and Nineveh, prophecy enabled the city to alter its behavior and avoid His judgment.

But it is possible to focus on the future so much that it distracts from immediate responsibilities. Many excuses are birthed while thinking about the road ahead and ignoring the needs of the present.

The Rehearsal or Living Life Live

Living in the future can include an unhealthy preoccupation with eschatology, the study of the Last Days. Some people become so fixated on what will take place that they fail to carry out Christ's commandments for the present. Jesus told His followers, **"Occupy till I come"** (Luke 19:13 KJV), meaning, "Until I return, continue to take care of My interests in the present."

DOOM AND GLOOM

While we may not resort to occult methods to discern or predict upcoming events, misuse of the prophetic feeds insecurity, which produces the kind of rehearsing the Lord instructed me to avoid.

Corrupted prophecy is rehearsing the future through a spirit of fear. The danger comes when it is used in an attempt to scare people into obedience. The Lord warned Barbara and me:

"By imagining worst case scenarios, you make things worse than they are. When you tell these things to other people, you instill fear and quench hope. That is not of Me.

"It is the prophet's way, when he is carnal, to assume fear can be a tool for righteousness. In fact, fear is a tool of the enemy. The tool I give to My servants is love, and you need to use it to draw people to Me.

"Be very careful not to resort to doom and gloom. Even if you use it to control someone for his best interest, it is still manipulation. When people see through it, they end up angry and farther away from Me.

Chapter 5 – Rehearsing Vs. Planning

"That is why the Gospel of the Kingdom is love and not fear. No one wants more to fear. Everyone wants to know they are loved.

"Only when love cares for a man's soul does he feel accepted and at peace. The lack of peace in the world today speaks of the lack of love. I want My children to change that."

Chapter 6

Living Life Live

Although God exists outside of time, we can only interact with Him in the present. He told Barbara and me:

"In the past, there is evidence of Me; and in the future, hope of Me. But I AM found in the present. That is 'living life live.'"

"Live" signifies a current condition, being engaged in what's happening now. That is how God wants us to live our lives.

To hide from the demands of the present, I replayed portions of the past. With it came regrets over things I did which produced shame, guilt and a sense of unworthiness. These thoughts put me in agreement with Satan the accuser, and disavowed the work of the cross, insinuating that my unrighteousness was more powerful than Jesus' sacrifice.

In an effort to direct the future, I rehearsed it. Confining life to my script kept me from receiving what God desired

Chapter 6 - Living Life Live

for me. It made my days predictable, even boring. It deadened me to the spontaneous and joyful nature of the Holy Spirit, and tempted me to believe I could accomplish my plans without God's help.

While doing these things, I neglected to seek God in the present – the only place to experience a relationship with Him.

MAGICAL THINKING

Taken to the extreme, hiding in the past or trying to control the future leads to a fantasy world of magical thinking, where reality is avoided. Gratification becomes an obsession without considering at whose expense. It is veiled entitlement.

Magical thinking is another form of rehearsing – living outside the moment until the activities of the present no longer seem relevant. It is a delusion of grandeur, a self-image which becomes an idol. And for the Christian, it is taking the Lord's name in vain – claiming His identity without reflecting His character.

This kind of fantasizing fits the description in II Corinthians 10:5 (ASV), where Paul portrays spiritual warfare as **"casting down imaginations, and every high thing that is exalted against the knowledge of God..."**

Magical thinking is a paradox. It ignores the fact that its aspirations are never fulfilled. It partners with pride and resorts to excuses to justify failure. It embodies the double-minded man, whom James described as **"like a wave of the sea driven and tossed by the wind.... unstable in all his**

The Rehearsal of Living Life Live

ways…. **Let not that man suppose that he will receive anything from the Lord"** (James 1:6-8 NKJV).

HOW DO WE PROCEED?

"The future is promised to no one," says the old adage. But God said in Jeremiah 29:11 that His plans are to give **"a future and a hope"** to His people. The Bible teaches fallen man to repent over his disobedient past and live as God's child in the present, so his future will be richly fulfilling with the One who created and loves his soul. God wants what is best for His children.

How often do we look elsewhere for a guarantee, as if the future could be purchased like the warranty for a product or service? Then, when we get what we want, we immediately try to figure out how to make it last so we will always have it. But nothing we can own lasts forever. In the long run, it will eventually fail. The Bible says love is the element of life which never fails (I Corinthians 13).

Chapter 7

Courage for the Kingdom

When Revelation 21:8 says the cowardly **"shall have their part in the lake which burns with fire and brimstone"** (NKJV), it is talking about people who are fearful. That is why the Lord told me to stop rehearsing the future. I was attempting to control it out of fear.

Did rehearsing make me cowardly in God's eyes? Even if not, was I failing to trust Him? I think so. The Lord was taking me to task over *why* I rehearsed more than *what* I rehearsed.

In my case, there were many more bad rehearsals than good ones. In bad rehearsals, fear provoked me to imagine the way I wanted things to happen. Then I tried to influence other people to conform to my desires.

In two of the Gospels, Jesus said to **"take no thought"** for the future. Matthew quoted Him, **"So don't be anxious about tomorrow. God will take care of your tomorrow too. Live one day at a time"** (6:34 TLB).

The Rehearsal or Living Life Live

This is the kind of courage God wants us all to develop – to let Him be in control and trust Him for the outcome. It's a matter of truly believing He has our best interest at heart.

A FUTURE WITHOUT FEAR?

Fear is an expression of unbelief. The Lord told us:

"Fear puts you out of touch with your faith, but it does not diminish it. Would I require you to walk by faith and not provide you the means to do so? Fear either makes it harder or easier to live by faith, according to how you respond to the fear.

"I want you to choose faith. Start today. Whenever you have a fearful thought, make a faith-filled declaration out loud. Recognize fear as a robber, not reality.

"Fear never runs out of bad things to frighten you with, but how many of them ever happen? Fear scares you with not knowing, and tempts you to trust yourself rather than Me. Fear paints an ugly face on everything and makes your world dark and lifeless.

"Fear cannot remove the nature I've put in you, but fear tries to usurp it by the father of lies, who rules through intimidation and deception. I've given you the nature of joy and peace, not as a place to hide but as a platform to decree from. You choose which voice to listen to."

JESUS' WARNINGS

As Christians, we want to see beyond headlines which report destruction and forecast desolation. Rather than be

Chapter 7 – Courage for the Kingdom

alarmed at the state of the world, we should be concerned about Jesus' reprimands to the churches in Revelation 2-3.

Along with the Laodicean Church being lukewarm, the Ephesian Church leaving its First Love is most disconcerting, especially in light of what the Lord said about the end of the age: **"The love of most will grow cold"** (Matthew 24:12 NIV). Fear steals our zeal, makes us lukewarm (apathetic), and causes us to leave our First Love.

What is our " First Love"? It is more than our initial infatuation with Jesus Himself. He told the Church at Ephesus to return to their initial works. "First Love" is not only *who* but *how* we loved at first.

Leaving our First Love doesn't have to imply unfaithfulness. Leaving our First Love denotes a loss of fervency and intensity.

Ever notice how new Christians, who have great enthusiasm for a faith they know very little about, are so good at leading people to the Lord? Their passion, more than their knowledge, influences others.

Rehearsing the future distracts us from our First Love. Fear erodes our enthusiasm, and the things which once made us passionate become routine or seem to lose their relevance altogether.

Doorway to Your First Love

If we don't rehearse the things to come, how should we regard them? The Lord told Barbara and me:

"When you think ahead, do so in anticipation of Me. This is the only sure way to ward off fear. And as you sense My presence in the present, learn to be still and draw near to Me. Lack of activity is not necessarily idleness – it is the opportunity our relationship needs to remain close.

"The enemy would rob you through guilt over appearing to be idle, but I encourage you to view it differently. See quiet time as a lack of distraction and not poor stewardship. Receive it as a blessing and pursue it as the doorway to your First Love."

STEEPED IN GOD – LIVING LIFE LIVE

Jesus instructed the churches to return to their First Love. One way Barbara and I do this is soaking in His presence – enjoying the Lord's closeness in the moment. It is an

Chapter 8 – Doorway to Your First Love

expression of worship and prayer, communing with Him while we seek His peace, rest, strength and intimacy.

The Lord gave us this soaking prayer, which is part of our daily devotional time:

"I commit my being to the grace and authority of the Almighty God, and request Him to work on me as I sit still. Perfect me as a saint. Instill in me Your attributes. Enlarge my capacity for faith. Make me a productive fruitbearer for Your Spirit. Rest Your peace in me so my eyes will always be on You. And teach me the joy of Your salvation."

PASSION FOR LIFE

Where love and devotion meet, passion forms. Without passion there is no vision, and without vision there is no life.

Leaving our First Love is losing our passion for living. Regrets over the past and fear of the future extinguish the fire of our passion.

Leaving our First Love creates opportunity for an orphan mind-set, belief in entitlement, magical thinking and a spirit of poverty. These are roadblocks to our destiny, mirages in the desert which lure us off course and cause us to die of thirst.

God's path of life is to believe He is who the Bible says He is. That is why the Jews were commanded to celebrate His goodness at the mandated feasts, which were called "rehearsals." They were forerunners of the things we will experience in the Kingdom of God.

The Rehearsal OR Living Life Live
LOVING GOD

Our purpose on Earth is to **"love the Lord your God with all your heart, soul, mind and strength"** (Deuteronomy 6:5, Matthew 22:37 NKJV) – to experience passion for God that will replace all fear from the enemy.

"Then one of the scribes came, and having heard them reasoning together, perceiving that He had answered them well, asked Him, 'Which is the first commandment of all?'

"Jesus answered him, 'The first of all the commandments is: "Hear, O Israel, the Lord our God, the Lord is one. And you shall love the Lord your God with all your heart, with all your soul, with all your mind, and with all your strength." This is the first commandment. And the second, like it, is this: "You shall love your neighbor as yourself." There is no other commandment greater than these.'

"So the scribe said to Him, 'Well said, Teacher. You have spoken the truth, for there is one God, and there is no other but He. And to love Him with all the heart, with all the understanding, with all the soul, and with all the strength, and to love one's neighbor as oneself, is more than all the whole burnt offerings and sacrifices.'

"Now when Jesus saw that he answered wisely, He said to him, 'You are not far from the Kingdom of God'" (Mark 12:28-34 NKJV).

Isn't that where we all want to be?

Worry is Rehearsing

The Rehearsal is a work in progress for me personally. I am still learning these concepts each time I reread what I wrote in this booklet. My real test came just after I finished the original manuscript. That is when I added this chapter.

It was Christmas week and my whole world seemed to plunge out of control. Barbara even wrote a verse about it:

It was three days before Christmas with no presents to give,
And fear we might lose the place where we live;
But God came through as He always does,
And our depression has melted into rapturous love.

REHEARSING POVERTY AGAIN

We had to renegotiate a loan against the equity in our home, and the bank told us it would double the interest rate because our debt ratio was too high. They could even reject our application and call in the entire outstanding balance. Barbara was upbeat and full of faith, but I was fearful.

The Rehearsal or Living Life Live

Forgetting everything the Lord taught me, I withdrew into survival mode, trying to anticipate all the negative possibilities so I could break my fall if we lost our house. Where would we move? How could we accomplish the Herculean task of downsizing? Would our home-based ministry continue?

I was rehearsing poverty again, big time.

Things seemed to get worse whenever Barbara and I talked to the bank. I started to panic and said we had to freeze our spending, which meant no Christmas gifts for our children and grandchildren. Worry made me uncharacteristically depressed. I couldn't sleep, had no appetite and was losing weight.

My rehearsing was the pride of leaning on my own understanding and spurning the wisdom of Proverbs 3:5-6 (NKJV)—

"Trust in the Lord with all your heart, and lean not on your own understanding; in all your ways acknowledge Him, and He shall direct your paths."

VISION OF A SWAMP

Barbara sensed my distress. She had a vision that I was wading through a swamp infested with many alligators. Elevated over the water she saw an observation walkway, like in the Everglades, where people can view the alligators in perfect safety. I was ignoring the protection of rising above my circumstances, and chose to put myself in danger.

Barbara reminded me again and again of how many times the Lord has come to our rescue. He has never forgot-

Chapter 9 - Worrying is Rehearsing

ten us in times of trouble. But I was becoming irrational and wouldn't receive her encouragement. I was having a full-dress rehearsal. Double-mindedness was making me crazy.

The Lord once said to me, *"If a man doesn't listen to his wife, he won't listen to Me either."* When I withdrew, I would not hear Barbara and could not hear God.

About a week before our crisis, the Lord told me:

"This is the season for your hearing to be fine-tuned. I'm directing you as I always have, but more will depend on your understanding and obedience in the days to come. So I will teach you to sort out the other voices and hear only Me. I'm not done with you yet, and I will teach you to hear Me exactly."

This was a classic example of a problem – an opportunity in work clothes.

BREAKTHROUGH

My mental malaise was still present at our final meeting with the bank officer. Our daughter, a real estate agent, gave us good advice and went with us. As it turned out, we were able to extend our loan at the existing interest rate. Everything turned out fine.

Leaving that meeting reminded me of a September evening long ago, when I responded to an altar call and surrendered my life to Jesus. I felt physically lighter, as if a great weight were lifted from my shoulders. I was more than happy, I was joyful. I felt good, not only because I was relieved but because God is faithful.

The Rehearsal or Living Life Live

Once the darkness dissolved, I wanted to learn from this experience so I wouldn't have to repeat it. The Lord showed me this fear was already inside me, and a crisis was necessary so it would be exposed. I prayed to be teachable, not only in my mind but in my spirit and physical body. I wanted my total being to be in agreement never to enter this place again.

SPIRITUAL ALIGNMENT

Every morning I say a prayer the Lord gave us for spiritual alignment:

"I command my spirit to be in charge of my being today and align itself with God's Spirit to do His will. I command my soul (emotions, personality, carnal nature) and my body (physical house, flesh) to submit to my spirit, and I call my being into agreement.

"I command my spiritual senses to engage: Spiritual eyes, see in the spirit. Spiritual ears, hear in the spirit. Spiritual heart, comprehend the things of the spirit. And I declare myself teachable. Holy Spirit, teach me today. In Jesus' name, amen."

I also put on the whole armor of God (Ephesians 6:11-17). How could I repeat these prayers daily and still fall into such a pit of despair? Fear got the better of me because the enemy scared me with facts so I would not see the truth that God loves me and has my best interest at heart.

Many years ago, the Lord instructed us, "Learn to trust Me now while it is still easy, because you won't be able to learn it when your world is falling apart." This word is more relevant today than ever.

Chapter 9 - Worrying is Rehearsing
OUR SEASON OF INCREASE

After leaving the bank, I went to pay the remainder of our property taxes, which were due by the end of the month. The clerk seemed puzzled at the computer screen and called her supervisor. They both looked confused. Then they told me, "Your taxes have already been paid. You don't owe us a cent."

I thought we owed over $2,000. On the way home, the Lord told me, *"You have entered your season of increase."*

Later that day, a stranger handed Barbara a Christmas card while she was shopping for presents. When our granddaughter opened it, there was $20 inside.

Another manifestation of increase came along with a healing. After nearly two years of using oxygen for a lung condition, Barbara is improving daily and breathing without it. That saves us at least $90 a month in equipment rental and electricity.

Every morning, I pray this prayer which the Lord gave me:

"I take authority over our finances. I declare, 'We have entered our season of increase, redemption, restoration and restitution, and I ask God to bring it to pass.'

"I claim the resources for our assignment. And I pray for our stewardship skills and the unhindered supply of heaven to be released to us for all our needs."

PRAYING FOR EACH OTHER

That evening, a dear friend – an 81-year-old Native American in California – called to say the Lord had him pray for us for several weeks. God specifically gave him Psalm 32:7

The Rehearsal or **Living Life Live**

(NKJV) to declare over us:

"You are my hiding place; You shall preserve me from trouble; You shall surround me with songs of deliverance."

Thank God for praying friends!

When I could reflect on this experience and draw conclusions, the Lord told me, *"You didn't lose your faith, you lost your mind."*

Double-mindedness rendered me vulnerable to the enemy and made me crazy because my thoughts were at war with each other. As in James 1:6-8, I could not receive anything from the Lord.

When I returned to my right mind, Jesus' words in Luke 12 took on fresh meaning—

"Therefore I say to you, do not worry about your life, what you will eat; nor about the body, what you will put on. Life is more than food, and the body is more than clothing.…

"And do not seek what you should eat or what you should drink, nor have an anxious mind. For all these things the nations of the world seek after, and your Father knows that you need these things. But seek the Kingdom of God, and all these things shall be added to you.

"Do not fear, little flock, for it is your Father's good pleasure to give you the Kingdom. Sell what you have and give alms; provide yourselves money bags which do not grow old, a treasure in the heavens that does not fail, where no thief approaches nor moth destroys. For where your treasure is, there your heart will be also" (22-23, 29-34 NKJV).

Chapter 10

A Personal Note

This booklet is an exercise in overcoming, which is more often a process than an event. I am encouraged by what Paul wrote to the Church in Philippi, **"He who began a good work in you will perfect it until the day of Jesus Christ"** (Philippians 1:6 NASB). God not only initiates the process but He is patient with it and with us.

Living life live – experiencing God in the present – is how we overcome our own sin issues and the snares of the world. John wrote in his first epistle, **"Everyone born of God overcomes the world. This is the victory that has overcome the world, even our faith"** (5:4 NIV).

Jesus told His disciples, **"Be of good cheer, I have overcome the world"** (John 16:33 NKJV). He wants us to follow Him as overcomers.

The Rehearsal or Living Life Live
RICHEST PROMISES

In chapters 2-3 of Revelation, following Jesus' reprimand to each church in Asia, some of the richest promises found anywhere in Scripture are made to "he who overcomes"—

"I will give the right to eat from the tree of life, which is in the Paradise of God" (2:7).

(He) **"will not be hurt at all by the second death"** (2:11).

"I will give some of the hidden manna. I will also give him a white stone with a new name written on it, known only to him who receives it" (2:17).

"I will give authority over the nations" (2:26).

(He will) **"be dressed in white. I will never blot out his name from the book of life, but will acknowledge his name before My Father and His angels"** (3:5).

"I will make him a pillar in the temple of My God. Never again will he leave it. I will write on him the name of My God and the name of the city of My God, the new Jerusalem, which is coming down out of heaven from My God; and I will also write on him My new name" (3:12).

"I will give the right to sit with Me on My throne, just as I overcame and sat down with My Father on His throne" (3:21).

And after the events of this book take place, Jesus promises that he who overcomes **"shall inherit all things, and I will be his God and he shall be My son"** (21:7 NKJV).

Chapter 10 – A Personal Note
TRUSTING GOD

By telling me not to rehearse the future, God is teaching me to walk in faith instead of fear. Part of faith is faithfulness, and part of faithfulness is timely obedience.

Just when I thought I had received all my concepts for *The Rehearsal*, and all the admonitions which came with them, I was reading about King Saul's disobedience in I Samuel 15. While giving the king God's specific instructions for attacking the Amalekites, the prophet said to **"utterly destroy all that they have, and do not spare them"** (v. 3 NKJV).

Saul laid siege and obeyed most of what God commanded, but he left their king unharmed and seized the choice animals of their flocks and herds. Samuel confronted him, saying, **"Rebellion is as the sin of witchcraft, and stubbornness is as iniquity and idolatry"** (v. 23 NKJV).

This verse unnerved me in a very profound way. "Stubbornness" is a biblical term for resisting God's will. In me, stubbornness was foot-dragging – passive-aggressive procrastination. Saul was stubborn and it cost him everything he had, including his life.

As I considered **"stubbornness is as iniquity and idolatry,"** I cringed at the thought that being slow to obey is construed as iniquity (perversity of heart) and idolatry (worshipping the god of Self).

God told Barbara and me to write our book *Things Hoped For* more than 20 years before we completed it. Much of the delay was because I didn't take the assignment seriously.

The Rehearsal or **Living Life Live**

He instructed me to produce *The Rehearsal* over nine months ago, and even told me what to name it. During that time I made some notes and organized an outline, but I didn't really jump in. Although this assignment opened my eyes to life- changing concepts I knew would help other people, I simply lacked the discipline to persevere.

Just before I started writing *The Rehearsal* in earnest, the Lord said to me:

"Trust Me. That's all I ask of you. You don't have to know the future. Plans are one thing; trying to see ahead out of fear in order to control is another.

"If you trust Me, you can live with peace in the present and have peace about the future. But you have to trust Me.

"As long as everything is comfortable and predictable, you can think you trust Me and say you trust Me when you really don't.

"I reward faithfulness. You're not being unfaithful, but you're not trusting Me. You're not giving your heart to Me as you should. I want you to do the best with what I've given you, and then you can ask Me to increase you in all these other ways that you're doubting.

"Don't look at other people's prophetic words as a way to avoid responsibility for what I Myself have told you to do. Recognize that I will tell you the important things you need to know for now.

"It's not that you can't learn and be blessed by

Chapter 10 - A Personal Note

prophetic words that come through other people. They will help you along the way. But in terms of what you're most accountable for, what you hear directly from Me is your first responsibility.

"Review what I Myself have given you to do. See what still needs to be done, what you've laid down that you need to pick up, and how you need to get your footing again on the assignment I've given you. Be faithful. Be engaged. Be loyal to Me. Be a son who wants to please. See Me rewarding you as the good and faithful servant you want to be.

"It is true that this is a new season. There are many new things, but don't be attracted to the new for novelty's sake. See how you can enter the new by being responsible for what you already know.

"Promotion comes easily in My Kingdom. You're not competing with anyone else. Promotion comes simply and solely by trusting Me.

"Don't try to earn your authority. Earned authority becomes works very quickly if you start doing things so you can be promoted, have more influence, do more, go more, be more. Instead, let the loyalty of your heart be toward Me.

"Let your desire to please Me and show your love for Me guide you through what you already know to do. Then, as more things become obvious in your assignment, you'll be equipped for them."

The Rehearsal or **Living Life Live**

TAKE THE CHALLENGE

My challenge, and yours if this booklet has spoken to you, is to rehearse God's faithfulness to us as individuals, and not allow fear of the future to encroach on our confidence in Him.

For those of us who look ahead to the greatest harvest of souls in history, fixing our gaze on God is essential. And to us who want to be found faithful and commended by our Heavenly Father, it is life.

"So we must get rid of everything that slows us down, especially the sin that just won't let go. And we must be determined to run the race that is ahead of us. We must keep our eyes on Jesus, who leads us and makes our faith complete" (Hebrews 12:1-2 CEV).